This book is dedicated to the fathers and father figures who show up, who teach by example, and who remind children that learning begins with love.

-JB

Written by Jawan Burwell
Illustrated by Passion Burnell
Edited by Shirley Faulkner-Springfield

ISBN (Hardcover): [979-8-9995307-0-7]
ISBN (Paperback): [979-8-9995307-1-4]
ISBN (E-book): [979-8-9995307-2-1]

Printed in the United States of America

Daddy's Classroom

A Journey Of Learning Together

Author: Jawan Burwell
Illustrator: Passion Burnell

In a bright and colorful classroom, the walls glowed like warm sunsets, and the floors were as soft as fluffy clouds. Children filled the room with laughter, building tall towers, painting colorful masterpieces, and reading books.

But this wasn't just any classroom. It was a magical place where dads were welcome too! Once a week, dads joined the fun -- building, playing, and exploring alongside their children. Together, they made every day a little more special and a lot more exciting!

Meet Marquis and his dad, Mr. Henry! Marquis always looked forward to the days his dad visited the classroom. Marquis called it "Daddy's Classroom" because these visits made learning extra special. Together, Marquis and Mr. Henry worked on puzzles, read stories, and played games, turning each visit into a new learning adventure.

"Daddy, look! We are building a tower with the blocks!" Marquis shouted in excitement as he stacked the blocks higher than himself.

Mr. Henry smiled and said, "Let's see how tall we can make it together.

Marquis knew his dad worked very hard, and sometimes, he couldn't visit the classroom because of work. But even when he couldn't be there in person, Mr. Henry always found a way to connect. One day, on the iPad, he read a story about superheroes to Marquis. With a warm voice full of excitement, Mr. Henry asked, "Which superhero do you think would save the day?"

After Marquis read the book on the iPad with his dad, Mr. Jordan played a superhero game with him. As a dedicated male preschool teacher, Mr. Jordan loved teaching, connecting with his students, and helping them grow. His enthusiasm, combined with Marquis's dad's visits, made the classroom feel like a truly special place to learn.

The preschool teachers were impressed by how involved Marquis's dad was, even with his busy schedule. Mr. Jordan often shared with the other teachers how important it was for dads to be engaged in their children's learning, even in small ways. "When dads join in, it makes a lasting impact," he said.

At home, Marquis and his dad found ways to keep learning fun. They would play basketball, read stories, and talk about what Marquis had learned at school.

At the end of the week, Mr. Jordan invited Mr. Henry to the classroom to talk about his job as a building contractor. He explained how he helped build schools, homes, and roads.

Marquis's friends were fascinated by his dad's story and had many questions for him. "What kind of tools do you use?" asked Jamal. Kiara wondered, "What do you like to build?"Jose asked, "Do you build towers like we do with the blocks?"

With a big smile, Mr. Henry answered all their questions, making everyone excited to learn about different ways people help the community.

Marquis beamed with pride after his dad said, "Helping to build things that make our community strong is my way of ensuring you have a bright future!" The children listened intently, fascinated because they knew someone who was building their community, and he was their friend's dad.

Mr. Henry felt proud. He knew that even though his job kept him busy, being part of Marquis's education helped make their bond stronger. He wasn't just a dad -- he was Marquis's hero!

Marquis's friends loved hearing about how involved his dad was and would tell their own dads all about his visits. Curious to see for themselves, they wanted to join in on the fun too.

Over the next few weeks, fathers who were dropping their children off at school noticed Marquis's dad engaging in the classroom. They saw the difference it was making and were inspired to be more engaged in their own children's learning.

As the months went by, the movement of Daddy's Classroom began to inspire preschools around the globe. Schools, teachers, and families witnessed a remarkable transformation as more fathers began to actively engage in the classroom with their children. Fathers became partners in learning, turning ordinary moments into extraordinary adventures.

The movement proved that when dads and father figures are involved, children thrive, families grow stronger, and the classroom becomes a shared space of joy, connection, and discovery.

As a male preschool teacher, Mr. Jordan encouraged dads to take part in reading stories, leading activities, and sharing their talents. Fathers introduced children to music, to building projects, and to careers, creating unique learning experiences. Mr. Jordan's classroom became famous for showing how much fathers and male role models matter. Their involvement not only enriched the classroom but also inspired other schools to embrace the value of engaged fatherhood in early education.

Now, in classrooms all over the world, dads, and father figures are not just visitors who drop their children off at school, they are a part of their children's learning journey. And children like Marquis know that "Daddy's Classroom" is the best classroom of all.

Let's Talk About Daddy's Classroom

Read these together and share your answers.

1. What was your favorite activity that Marquis did with his dad?

2. How does your dad or a male role model help you when you try something new?

3. Marquis's dad showed the children how he helps the community. How could you help someone at school or home?

4. How can you show up for your friends, just like in Daddy's Classroom?

A Promise to Fathers and Father Figures

We promise that the classroom sees you.
Not as a helper.
Not as a visitor.
But as a teacher in your child's first lessons and
a steady presence in moments that matter.
These pages honor the many ways fatherhood
shows up—through patience, curiosity,
consistency, and care.
Whether you are learning as you go, balancing
long days, or simply doing your best,
your presence makes a difference.
You do not have to be perfect.
You just have to be present.
This classroom was made with you in mind.
Your voice belongs here, and your child learns
differently because you are here.

"The greatest lessons are taught not by words alone,
but by showing up."
—Dr. Jawan Burwell

My father gave me the greatest gift anyone could give another person, he believed in me.

-Jim Valvano

About the Author

Dr. Jawan Burwell, Ed.D., is an educator, author, and advocate for fathers and father figures who show up in their children's lives. He holds a Bachelor's in Child Development and Family Studies from North Carolina A&T State University, a Master's in Youth, Family, and Community Sciences from North Carolina State University, and a Doctor of Education from Walden University. As a preschool program director, Dr. Burwell has spent years creating and leading learning environments where children thrive. He believes that learning begins not just in the classroom, but in everyday moments where curiosity, guidance, and presence come together. Through Daddy's Classroom, he celebrates the fathers, mentors, and role models who inspire children to explore, learn, and grow. He resides in North Carolina, where he continues developing opportunities for children and fathers to learn, grow, and explore together.

www.ingramcontent.com/pod-product-compliance
Ingram Content Group UK Ltd.
Pitfield, Milton Keynes, MK11 3LW, UK
UKHW060119010826
14089UKWH00005B/57

9 798999 530707